FIRST-PERSON STORIES OF

9/11

BY NICOLE HORNING

ROSEN PUBLISHING PRIMARY SOURCE LIBRARY

ROSEN PUBLISHING

Published in 2027 by The Rosen Publishing Group, Inc.
2544 Clinton Street, Buffalo, NY 14224

Designer: Deanna Lepovich
Editor: Nicole Horning

Cataloging-in-Publication Data

Names: Horning, Nicole.
Title: First-person stories of 9/11 / Nicole Horning.
Description: Buffalo, NY : Rosen Publishing, 2027. | Series: The Rosen Publishing primary source library | Includes glossary and index.
Identifiers: ISBN 9781725342897 (pbk.) | ISBN 9781725342903 (library bound) | ISBN 9781725342910 (ebook)
Subjects: LCSH: September 11 Terrorist Attacks, 2001–Juvenile literature. | United States–History–21st century–Juvenile literature.
Classification: LCC E893.H67 2027 | DDC 909.83–dc23

Manufactured in the United States of America

CPSIA Compliance Information: Batch #CSRYA27. For further information, contact Rosen Publishing at 1-800-237-9932.

CONTENTS

FOREWORD

History is so much more than just a boring collection of names and dates. It is a collection of stories—sometimes tragic stories, sometimes heroic stories, sometimes romantic stories, sometimes scary stories. And they're all stories of real people who lived real lives.

Those stories can get lost in the shuffle of memorizing battles, studying maps, and listing important court cases or rulers. That's why primary sources are so valuable. They remind us that historical events happened to and because of real people. Reading diaries, looking at photographs, and seeing newspaper articles are just some ways to make history feel personal through primary sources.

Another way is through watching or listening to interviews with people who lived through major historical events. That's what you're invited to do in this book—and all the books that are part of the *Rosen Publishing Primary Source Library*. Each chapter includes quotes from an interview with a real person who experienced a major historical event in a deeply personal way. You can also scan the QR code included at the beginning of each chapter to watch a video interview with the person featured in that chapter.

Created in partnership with Generations Broadcasting, the *Rosen Publishing Primary Source Library* was created to remind readers that there is power in sharing our stories. First-person stories make history come alive. And when history comes alive, we're better able to learn from it—and avoid the mistakes of the past.

The events you're living through today will be part of the next generation's history lessons. As you read and watch the stories collected here, think about what you want your story to be.

Note: More interviews about the topics featured in this series, as well as many other historical events, can be accessed via a subscription to Rosen Publishing's GBC Stories Database: rosendigital.com/GBCStories/.

HOW TO WATCH THE INTERVIEWS FEATURED IN THIS BOOK

- Use your phone's camera, and hold it over the QR code.
- Click the link that appears.
- Watch the video that pops up. If you would like to read a transcript of the interview while you watch, you can click on that option in the video's menu.

INTRODUCTION

People remember exactly where they were on the morning of September 11, 2001. Some were in classrooms, others were on the subway, and many were watching television when the unthinkable happened: Airplanes crashed into the Twin Towers of the World Trade Center, the Pentagon, and a field in Pennsylvania. For most Americans, that day, often referred to now as simply 9/11, began like any other. But by the end, lives had been lost, heroes had emerged, and a nation was changed forever.

On that day, 19 people **hijacked** 4 passenger airplanes that were supposed to fly from the East Coast to California. These people, who were **terrorists**, turned the planes into weapons by purposefully flying them into buildings. Two of these planes hit the World Trade Center Twin Towers.

American Airlines Flight 11 hit the North Tower at 8:46 a.m. while United Airlines Flight 175 hit the South Tower at 9:03 a.m. Because of damages from the impacts and the fires they caused, both towers completely collapsed within two hours after the first plane hit the North Tower. During this time, between 16,400 and 18,000 people in the World Trade Center complex rushed to **evacuate** the buildings while first responders such as firefighters rushed in to save people who were trapped or injured. Many people in the complex were able to safely leave, but thousands still lost their lives.

American Airlines Flight 77 hit the Pentagon, which is the headquarters of the United States Department of Defense located in Arlington, Virginia, at 9:37 a.m. The fourth plane crashed into an empty field near Shanksville, Pennsylvania, at 10:02 a.m., because passengers and crew members on the flight learned about the other attacks and fought back against the hijackers to prevent the plane from reaching its target. Many believe the target for this fourth plane was either the White House or the Capitol in Washington, D.C.

The terrorists were part of an Islamist **extremist** group called al-Qaeda. They believed religion should be the foundation for a country's laws, culture, and social lives, and that it was necessary to use violence to reach their goals. It's important to note that most Muslims do not share these beliefs.

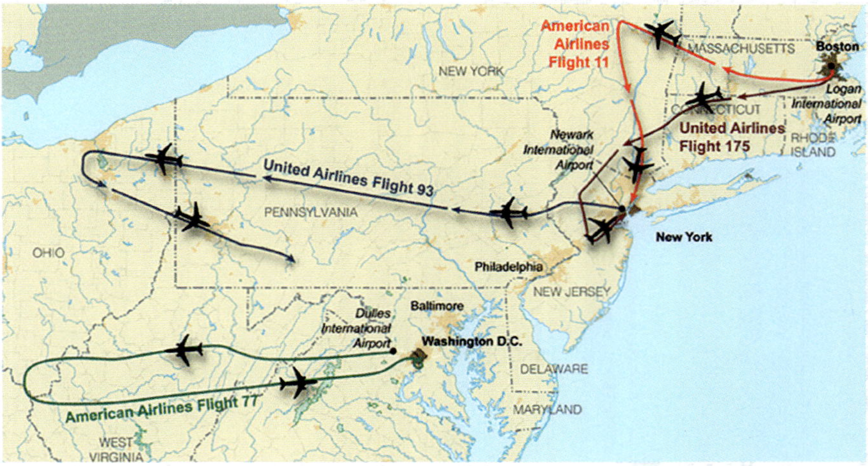

This map shows the flight path for all four planes on September 11. It includes where the planes left from and where they crashed.

In New York City, 2,753 people died as a result of the World Trade Center attacks, 184 people died at the Pentagon, and 40 people died on Flight 93 when it crashed in Pennsylvania.

The attacks led to big changes in the United States. For the first time in history, all commercial flights were grounded, and safety rules were added that airports still follow today. The U.S. government expanded its efforts to keep citizens safe by creating the Department of Homeland Security. Many of the ways we travel, communicate, and protect public spaces were shaped by the events of 9/11.

The events of 9/11 also affected many different communities. Families lost loved ones, and survivors carry memories of fear and loss that have stayed with them. Many Muslims, Arab Americans, **Sikh** Americans, and other groups faced **discrimination** after the attacks, even though they had nothing to do with terrorist groups. Learning about this history helps us know how important it is to treat others fairly and not judge them based on their religion or background.

More than two decades later, 9/11 continues to shape American life. Museums, memorials, and annual remembrance ceremonies honor the people who died, the first responders who went into the towers when everyone else was trying to leave, and the communities that rebuilt afterward. By learning about this day and the stories of those who lived through it, we can better understand how one day can change a nation and why it's important to remember what happened. Through firsthand stories, historical information, and critical-thinking questions, you'll learn what happened that day and why it still matters today.

CHAPTER ONE

IT BEGAN LIKE ANY OTHER DAY

September 11 began as any other day. Children got ready to go to school, and adults got ready to go to work. Everyone followed their typical morning **routine**, not realizing that the day was unlike any other and would become a part of history. Even decades later, people remember where they were and what they were doing when the planes hit the Twin Towers.

All the events of that day were easily remembered by people even many years later because they were so frightening to watch from afar on TV screens and experience in the moment as people in New York City, Arlington, and Shanksville did. David is one of those people who vividly remember all the details of his day on 9/11.

THE FIRST SIGNS SOMETHING WAS WRONG

David started his workday thinking it was going to be like any other: reading the newspaper on the train, paying attention to the time because he was going to be late for work. The difference between David and many other adults in the United States on September 11 is that he worked in New York City, near the Twin Towers. In his interview,

Scan this QR code to watch David talk about his experience on 9/11, which started just like any other workday.

The Twin Towers, shown here in 1995, were some of the tallest buildings in the world.

he explains how his day started and his experience encountering the beginning of the attacks:

> *So as always, I was running late ... I was reading the* Wall Street Journal *that morning, as I always did ... It was about some protests that were gonna take place a few weeks later. The World Trade Organization and the IMF and World Bank had had all kinds of very big protests happening at the meetings that they had around the world. I finished the article as the train pulled into the World Trade Center. I looked at my watch. It was 8:54 ... When I got out of the car, the doors open. I kind of looked around and I smelled ... Did a diesel engine come through here? And this was all electric. It was the subway. Something was wrong, and I could smell fumes that were not supposed to be in the basement of the World Trade Center ... There were a few little stores down in that little concourse area, and there were fire alarms going off, but nobody was changing what they were doing ... I kind of looked around and I thought, all right, I mean, maybe there's a little fire. I don't know. I smelled smoke.*

An automated camera set up in Brooklyn captured Flight 11 hitting the North Tower, which can be seen in this series of photographs.

Like many in the city, David didn't completely understand what was happening. What David and many other people didn't know was that a plane had hit the North Tower approximately 8 minutes before, at 8:46. The North Tower had 110 floors, and the plane hit between floors 93 and 99. The impact immediately caused

The World Trade Center is shown here shortly after the planes hit the towers. Holes and fires in the buildings can be seen.

FAST FACT

IN 1993, THE WORLD TRADE CENTER EXPERIENCED ITS FIRST TERRORIST ATTACK, WHICH AT THAT TIME WAS THE DEADLIEST TERRORIST ACT IN U.S. HISTORY. IN FEBRUARY 1993, A TRUCK BOMB EXPLODED IN THE BASEMENT PARKING GARAGE OF THE NORTH TOWER, INJURING MORE THAN 1,000 PEOPLE AND KILLING 6.

fires, which caused the diesel and smoke smells that David noticed.

EARLY MOMENTS OF UNCERTAINTY

The impacts of the planes on the towers shook the buildings and surrounding areas and created a large exploding sound. After the 1993 attack on the World Trade Center towers, people who were there back then and remembered the event were

When the towers collapsed, steel and other debris fell onto buildings and spread throughout the area.

PHONES AND TRANSPORTATION ISSUES ON 9/11

After the planes hit the Twin Towers, many families immediately tried to get in contact with their loved ones, especially those they knew in New York City. However, many people found it difficult to contact their loved ones because the attacks had destroyed cell towers, and the remaining cell towers and networks were overloaded with millions of calls all at one time. This caused the networks to crash, making it nearly impossible for people to reach their loved ones.

In addition to phone networks crashing, public transport was shut down in New York City. Bridges and subway lines were shut down, and other traffic restrictions were put into place, which made it difficult to get into or out of the city.

These shutdowns and overloaded networks meant people couldn't travel into the city to find their loved ones and they couldn't reach their loved ones on the phone, which added to the panic and stress of the day. Many survivors who made it out of the towers had to figure out how to get home that day because of transportation and bridges being completely shut down. The solution available to them was to walk home.

Shlomo Yadoo, who worked in the North Tower for the Port Authority, walked 15 miles (24 km) home. Linda Raisch-Lopez worked on the 97th floor of the South Tower. She walked down all those flights of stairs barefoot then walked 3.5 miles (5.6 km) in her high heels to the ferry at the Hudson River pier. She didn't realize her feet were blistered and bloody until she reached the ferry because her focus was on getting home. Her shoes are on display at the 9/11 Memorial and Museum.

immediately prepared to leave if they felt **threatened**. So shortly after the hit of the first plane, people started to evacuate—even people like David who had just arrived. This created a lot of confusion and shock, and as David said in his interview, he thought the protests he had read about on the train were already happening:

> *As I always did, I went to the stairs to run up, and as I was going up the stairs ... the private security guys in the World Trade Center are telling people go out the door, go out to the right ... When I got to the top of the stairs, I see these*

people directing us to our right. And I looked over my right shoulder and I just read this article about these protests, and I thought they're burning papers in this lobby—I could see into the World Trade Center lobby—and there's smoke and I see papers on fire and I thought, 'What's going on? I mean, I just read this article, are they protesting here already?'

Initial reactions to the impact of the first plane on the North Tower were that it was an accident. Many people thought a plane flying so low and fast was because the pilot had poor flying skills, or it was a small plane accidentally hitting the tower. Even the first responders and others who saw the first plane hit the North Tower were confused.

Debris from the towers coated trucks, buildings, and city streets.

Ruins of the collapsed towers are shown here.

PAPERS FALLING LIKE SNOW

When the plane hit the North Tower, along with a loud and jarring noise, a lot of **debris** fell from the affected floors. David and others around the towers saw the papers and other debris falling out of the building. They looked at the plane sticking out of the tower in **disbelief**:

> *I start to walk out, and as we come out of the mall area in between the two World Trade Center buildings, I see papers flying in the sky and it looked like someone had taken a blowtorch to a filing cabinet. All the papers were charred*

FAST FACT

THE BURNED PAPERS THAT WERE EJECTED FROM THE SHATTERED WINDOWS WERE CARRIED FOR MILES ON THE WIND THROUGHOUT NEW YORK CITY'S BOROUGHS. MANY OF THESE PAPERS WERE CLEARED AWAY, BUT SOME WERE RECOVERED BY PEOPLE AND ARE NOW **PRESERVED** IN THE 9/11 MEMORIAL AND MUSEUM.

on the outside. The middle of the paper was perfectly intact. [We] just see this snowstorm of paper flying, and somebody said an airplane hit the World Trade Center ...

'Yeah, an airplane hit the World Trade Center. There's no way. Why would that ever happen?' And I look up over my left shoulder and I see flames shooting out of the building.

The force of the plane hitting the tower along with explosions that occurred because of the impact caused papers to be ejected out of the shattered office windows. The Twin Towers had many financial, legal, insurance, and other businesses housed there. Because of these offices and all the papers they each had (this was before documents were mostly kept online), the papers and other furnishings were a fuel source for the fires in the towers. These materials allowed the fires to spread through several floors and burn for a long time.

TRAGEDY BROADCAST ON LIVE TV

About 17 minutes after the plane hit the North Tower, another plane crashed into the South Tower between floors 77 and 85, trapping people who worked in the building on the floors above. The debris from this impact spread throughout the area, with the plane's engine falling to the ground about six blocks away. In his interview, David described the feeling of the plane hitting the South Tower. Even blocks away from the World Trade Center Towers, he was able to feel the massive impact:

I walked by the exchange. I went down a little alley that I always went to, and as I stepped into the deli,

FAST FACT

PRESIDENT GEORGE W. BUSH WAS READING TO AN ELEMENTARY SCHOOL CLASSROOM WHEN HE WAS TOLD OF THE SECOND PLANE HITTING THE SOUTH TOWER AT 9:05 A.M. HE MADE THE DECISION TO STAY CALM AND NOT JUMP UP AND SCARE THE CHILDREN BECAUSE HE KNEW THE FIRST THING A LEADER HAS TO DO IS STAY CALM. HE WAS ON A FLIGHT IN AIR FORCE ONE ON THE WAY TO NEW YORK CITY BY 9:55 A.M.

The events of 9/11 made headlines around the world, as can be seen in this collection of newspapers.

the second plane hit at this point ... I've never felt fear or shake like that in my life. It was a sound and a feeling that I'll never forget ... You could not see the World Trade Center from there, because it was deep in the canyons of Wall Street. It was probably six blocks away, but we were being showered and pelted by pieces of glass and metal ... Everybody was in a kind of panic. Now, at that point, I was going in a back entrance to the exchange. There were four buildings that made up the exchange. I was in one that was on Broad Street ... and as I walked into the building, they said, we're evacuating everybody out.

At approximately 8:48 a.m., two minutes after the North Tower was hit, news coverage started showing the scene at the World Trade Center, with many networks interrupting their regularly scheduled programming to cover the events. Because these networks were showing live footage, many people at home and in school tuned into their TVs just as confused and in shock as those in New York City. This also meant that millions of people saw when the second plane crashed into the South Tower, and everyone suddenly realized that the first crash wasn't an accident. These were attacks.

HOW YOU SEE HISTORY

1. Why do you think so many people remember exactly where they were and what they were doing on 9/11, even many years later? What does this tell us about the impact of historical events?
2. How did David's experience in New York City reflect how confusing the early moments of 9/11 were for people in the city?
3. How might seeing the second plane hit the South Tower on live TV change how people across the country understood the events of 9/11?

CHAPTER TWO

CHAOS AND LOSS

Many New Yorkers struggled to understand what was happening on 9/11. What caused this? How were people going to get out? And for many people in the city, were their loved ones okay? David and many others were in shock at what was happening around them: the dust clouds, the very loud bangs of explosions, people screaming, the deafening rumble of the towers collapsing, and then later, silence.

It was hard for anyone to process what was happening before their eyes, including those who were watching the events on TV. Many schools stopped lessons for the day and turned on the TV. Adults turned on the TV at home, which stayed on for most of the day. It was hard for anyone to process the events, in addition to the fear they were experiencing. In another part of David's interview, he describes his feelings in the city that day, from leaving the World Trade Center Complex to seeing one of the towers fall, and watching TV with his aunt like so many others in America that day.

A SEA OF PAPER

When the towers collapsed, the destruction didn't stay in one place. It spread throughout the area, and many buildings

Scan this QR code to watch David tell his story of watching the towers fall in front of him and his thoughts when watching footage on TV later that day.

The impact and heat from the planes twisted and destroyed steel columns in the towers. Recovered steel columns are shown here in the 9/11 Memorial and Museum.

around the World Trade Center were damaged or covered in debris. Streets that were normally busy were hard to **navigate** because of the falling papers, smoke, dust, and falling ash. David remembers what it was like to be in the area as he tried to make his way to safety:

> *We're over on the East River, and you could see the river filling up with paper ... It was huge sheets of paper that are just flying everywhere, ashes flying. The smoke was starting to be very* ***palpable****. It was just, something very wrong. I ran into two other people that I knew, and I said, "Guys let's get out of here." ... So we started walking*

FAST FACT

MANY OF NEW YORK CITY'S TV AND RADIO TOWERS WERE LOCATED ON TOP OF THE TWIN TOWERS. WHEN THE TOWERS COLLAPSED, MOST STATIONS WENT OFF THE AIR.

Papers from offices inside the Twin Towers were carried for miles on the wind. A city street with papers and cars coated with dust is shown here.

The collapse of the towers also damaged nearby buildings.

> *North. We got on ... FDR Drive, and the only thing I can think of at this point is that there's 30,000 or 50,000 people in those buildings. How can they possibly get out? Now, at the same time I left, my friends ... were stuck in the exchange. They were not allowed to leave. Certain buildings did certain things. There were four buildings connected. The building I tried to come in evacuated. The main room did not let anybody out.*

The situation around the towers was unpredictable and confusing. People didn't know where to go for safety from the falling towers, debris, and dust clouds. They also experienced uncertainty, not knowing if the building they sought safety in was safe. Some buildings ordered immediate evacuations, while others kept workers inside, unsure what may happen next. All around the neighborhood, papers from offices, broken glass, and dust covered the streets and drifted across the river.

NEWS SPREADS OF MORE ATTACKS

People escaped from the area around the towers however they could, which often meant walking in the middle of roads that were normally packed with cars. In an area as busy as New York City, this is one of the signs that something was very wrong. David remembered the moment he knew the attacks were part of something much larger than what he had just seen:

> *We started walking up FDR Drive, and we were in the middle of the FDR Drive, which is typically loaded with traffic. The only traffic on that road was heading south, and it was all emergency vehicles. It was ambulances, fire trucks. Everything kind of stopped and you realized that something different was happening. So as we're walking up literally the middle of the FDR Drive ... somebody at that time had a Blackberry ... and they received an email that the Pentagon had been hit.*

The damage to the Pentagon after the plane crash on 9/11 is shown here.

Some fire trucks and ambulances were crushed when the towers collapsed. The 9/11 Memorial and Museum has some of these trucks on display, like the one shown here.

FAST FACT

ASBESTOS WAS ONE OF THE MATERIALS USED DURING THE CONSTRUCTION OF THE TWIN TOWERS IN THE 1960S AND 1970S. IT WAS A HEAT-RESISTANT MATERIAL BUT IS KNOWN TODAY TO BE VERY HARMFUL AND LEAD TO HEALTH PROBLEMS SUCH AS CANCER. WHEN THE TOWERS COLLAPSED, THIS HARMFUL MATERIAL WAS RELEASED INTO THE AIR.

That was the point where we all realized this is an act of war. We have now seen something that none of us have ever experienced in our lives. We knew something really bad was happening, and the panic kind of set in.

For many people in New York, information came in slowly and unevenly. Many didn't realize there was an attack on the Pentagon and a **thwarted** attack that ended in Pennsylvania at 10:02 a.m.

until much later that day because a lot of the news was focused on the World Trade Center attacks. David's walk north happened at the same time the rest of the country was learning more about the attacks he escaped from.

At 9:37 a.m., another hijacked plane crashed into the Pentagon, which David learned on his walk to his aunt and uncle's apartment, which he said was about 5 miles (8 km) from the World Trade Center.

THE DUST CLOUD

When the towers collapsed, a huge gray cloud rose where the buildings stood. In that moment, no one knew how many people had escaped or were still inside. David described this moment in his interview:

This picture shows the Twin Towers collapsing and the dust cloud that formed in the process.

FAST FACT

FOR DAYS AFTER THE ATTACKS, RESIDENTS DESCRIBED WALKING THROUGH THE CITY LIKE "WALKING THROUGH A CLOUD," BECAUSE THE DUST FROM THE COLLAPSE DIDN'T SETTLE. SIMPLE THINGS LIKE GOING OUTSIDE TO GO TO WORK OR SCHOOL BECAME DANGEROUS.

When we were on FDR Drive ... that was when the first building came down. And I remember turning around and looking back and just tears welling up in my eyes thinking 30,000 people just died. That building is gone. I mean, it was unbelievable to think that something like that would happen. You just saw it come down.

When the towers collapsed, they created a massive dust cloud filled with dangerous materials and could be seen from far away. This photograph, which was taken from a distance, can help you visualize the size of the dust cloud.

LONG-TERM HEALTH PROBLEMS

Being near the dangerous and toxic dust cloud on 9/11 led to health problems that continue to affect people. In addition to mental effects such as **post-traumatic stress disorder (PTSD)**, **depression**, and **anxiety**, many people continue to experience asthma and other respiratory illnesses, ongoing headaches, and a variety of cancers.

These illnesses impact those who worked in the buildings as well as the first responders. By 2006, several dozen first responders had been diagnosed with cancer. Many doctors who examined them determined that their cancers were likely caused by the dangerous **particles** they were exposed to on 9/11. As of 2025, nearly 50,000 people have been diagnosed with cancer related to 9/11, and more than 6,000 people have died, which is more than the number of people who lost their lives on the day of the attacks.

The U.S. government created special programs to help these survivors and responders. The World Trade Center Health Program provides free medical care and monitors the health of people affected. Victims can also receive financial help through the September 11th Victim Compensation Fund.

Doctors and scientists continue to study the long-term effects of 9/11 to better understand how exposure to toxic dust affects the body. Their research helps improve treatments for survivors and first responders. Families and communities also work together to remember those who were lost and to support those still dealing with health problems today. This shows that the impact of 9/11 continues, even more than two decades later.

Firefighters spent a long time searching for people after the towers collapsed.

First responders and others are shown here wading through the debris from the collapse of the towers.

And I was several miles away at the time when it happened, but I could only imagine what was going on. I had really no idea what it meant, how many people had gotten out, what the gravity of it was, but it was not good.

The dust cloud was suffocating and made up of a dangerous and toxic mix of concrete, glass fibers, paint, soot, steel, jet fuel fumes, asbestos, and other dangerous building materials. The dust cloud made it hard for people to breathe or even see. The texture of the cloud was a fine powder, with the smallest pieces being the most dangerous because they were easier to inhale and get into the lungs.

Once the cloud settled, it laid on top of nearby buildings, especially in the financial district where David worked, and it was a few inches thick. The dust was moved by cleanup efforts after the attacks, wind, and people moving through the area, which **exposed** even more people in the city to the harmful dust for months.

FEAR, CONFUSION, AND LOSS

After the towers collapsed, communication across New York City became extremely difficult. Many TV and radio stations suddenly went off the air because their broadcast antennas had been located on top of the World Trade Center. People relied on whatever stations were still working. Like many others that day, David went to be with his closest family and turned on the TV:

> *All the communication towers were on the World Trade Center. The only station that was still broadcasting was WCBS, because they had a backup tower on the Empire State Building. Everybody else had towers downtown. So we turned it on, and we were watching what was happening ...*

The people shown here reacting to the aftermath of the attacks represent the fear and shock many experienced on and after 9/11.

and at this point I didn't know when I was gonna get home ... My Aunt Lynn and I sat and we watched and we cried, and we didn't know what it meant ... I had no contact with anybody at work, I had no way of getting in touch with them. At that point I could only assume that some of my best friends were gone.

When the towers fell, thousands of people inside the buildings were trapped, and many lost their lives. The destruction of communication systems made it nearly impossible for families, friends, and coworkers to know if their loved ones were safe. David's experience of having no contact with anyone from work reflects what countless people faced that morning: uncertainty, fear, and the desperate need for information. Many families

Many communication towers were on top of the World Trade Center. A part of the destroyed North Tower radio and television antenna is shown here.

After the collapse, debris spread throughout the area and ruins continued to smoke for days.

wouldn't learn the fate of their loved ones for hours or even days. The attacks destroyed physical buildings and changed the lives of thousands of people.

HOW YOU SEE HISTORY

1. Do you think it is important for government-funded health programs and compensation funds to exist for those affected by the events of 9/11?
2. What does 9/11 teach us about resilience during disasters?
3. How did the media coverage shape people's understanding of the attacks on that day?

CHAPTER THREE

AIR TRAVEL COMES TO A HALT

After the attacks on 9/11, the skies suddenly fell quiet and would stay like that for a few days. Air traffic across the nation was ordered to stop, which marked the first time this happened in U.S. history. Thousands of flights were grounded, which meant they couldn't fly, and airports quickly filled with stranded passengers. People like Ralph, whose story you'll discover in this chapter, had planned trips and were left waiting, wondering when they'd be able to fly again.

STRANDED IN THE SKIES

At 9:06 a.m., three minutes after the second plane hit the South Tower, airspace around New York City was shut down, with all flights ordered to land at the closest airport. However, minutes after the Pentagon attack, at 9:45 a.m., U.S. airspace was officially shut down across the entire nation, and all passenger flights had to immediately land. But not everyone was aware of what was happening in New York City and at the Pentagon. Ralph, a float plane pilot in Alaska, was unaware of what happened in New York City when he took off for a trip:

I took off on a float plane out of Anchorage, Alaska, heading out for a hunting and

Scan this QR code to watch Ralph tell his story of how 9/11 affected his life.

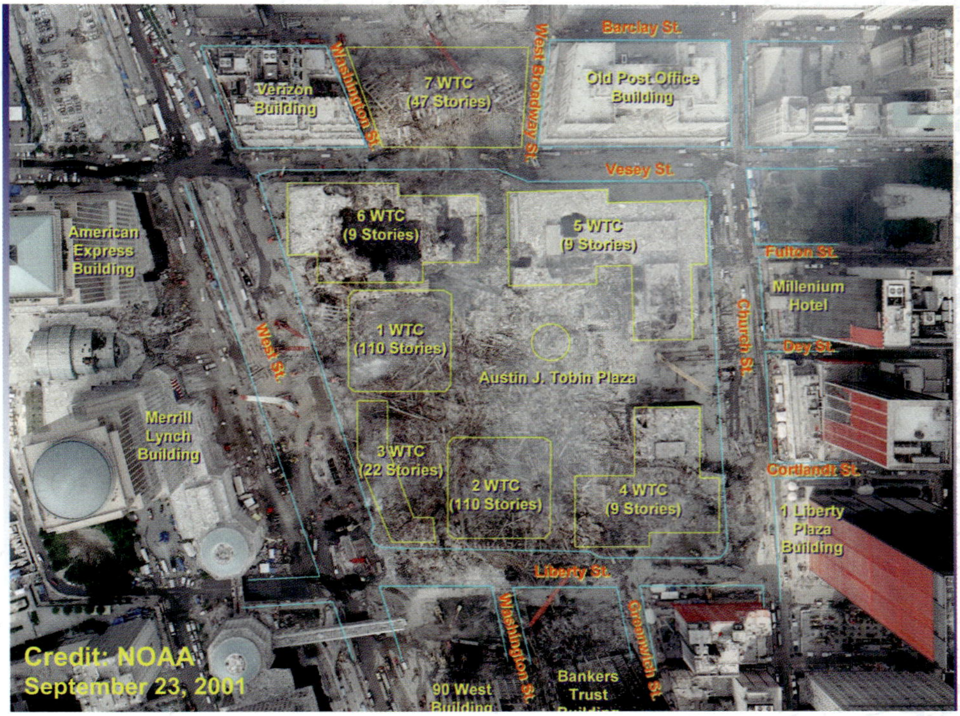

An overhead view of the damage and where the Towers and other buildings used to be is shown here.

fishing trip. We were airborne when it happened. We didn't know what had happened, but the next thing we knew, there was an F-16 fighter plane next to us telling us to land and don't come back up. We landed the plane and we sat there until he got a communication and said, "I'm sorry sir but you can't fly." We had to sit there for several days because we couldn't fly, and then finally they called and said, "You can fly, but you've got to go pick up a couple of caribou hunters who went out for a one-day hunt ... that was five days ago, and they had no supplies so they allowed us to fly to where they were to go pick them up and then fly back to Anchorage.

FAST FACT

ON 9/11, NEW YORK CITY'S 911 OPERATORS RECEIVED OVER 35,000 CALLS IN JUST A FEW HOURS, WHICH WAS MORE THAN TRIPLE A TYPICAL DAY.

COME FROM AWAY

When the U.S. Federal Aviation Administration (FAA) made the decision to shut down all U.S. airspace, more than 4,000 planes were forced to land at the nearest airport. Flights that were coming into the United States from Europe were forced to land in Canada. Gander International Airport in Newfoundland, Canada, received 38 planes filled with more than 6,500 passengers.

The town of Gander is very small, with a population of 10,000 people, which made finding shelter for all these additional people very difficult. Passengers were taken to schools, community centers, and Salvation Army centers in Gander and towns nearby.

This story inspired the musical *Come From Away*. The musical shows how people's differences clashed and separated them at first, but then this large group of strangers grew to trust each other, leading to lasting friendships. The friendships that started while people were stranded highlight what was going on in the world at the time. The world was experiencing a lot of fear and uncertainty after the attacks, but this large group of people was welcomed into the small town and learned to get along, even through their differences and stressful situations. The musical teaches us that kindness is important and can bring people together, especially during hard times.

***Come From Away* is a musical that tells the true story of stranded travelers on 9/11.**

Airports across the country were filled with people waiting. In larger cities like Chicago and Los Angeles, stranded travelers slept on the floors, lined up for food and water, and tried to stay informed as air traffic controllers worked to maintain safety while the nation processed the attacks.

EMPTY SKIES

The most unusual things to result from airspace closing was the silence and lack of contrails. For the caribou hunters that Ralph had to pick up, it was even scarier because they were unaware of the attacks in New York City and the safety measures that resulted from them. Ralph recalled their reaction to the empty skies:

> *These guys were terrified because Anchorage is a sky full of contrails ... these poor guys thought the world had come to an end because all of a sudden there were no contrails in the sky, there were no airplanes, and they were starving.*

Contrails are shown here. The empty sky without contrails was a reminder of how much had changed in a few days.

Days after the attacks, the ruins of the Twin Towers continued to smoke, showing that nothing was returning to normal.

The empty skies were a reminder of how much life had changed in those first few days after 9/11, even as everyone was still trying to understand what had happened. The normal patterns of everyday life, such as planes crossing the sky or people traveling for work or vacation, had suddenly gone away.

FAST FACT

A CONTRAIL IS A CLOUD-LIKE STREAM IN THE SKY MADE UP OF ICE CRYSTALS, WHICH IS FORMED BY AIRPLANES. WHEN AIRSPACE WAS CLOSED ON 9/11 AND THE DAYS AFTERWARD, THE CONTRAILS PEOPLE WERE USED TO SEEING WERE MISSING.

WATCHING FROM HOME

While some were stranded in airports, millions of Americans were watching the events unfold from their TV. Families watched news reports of closed airspace, emergency measures, and cleanup efforts in the affected areas. Many realized the attacks weren't just a tragedy, but a national emergency that affected ordinary people in ways they hadn't expected.

In the days following the attacks, authorities worked to reopen the skies, but safety remained a top priority. Flights slowly resumed with new security measures, and passengers began returning to their destinations. The grounded flights of 9/11 showed how interconnected the nation was and how quickly even ordinary travel could be disrupted by a major event.

HOW YOU SEE HISTORY

1. How did the events of 9/11 affect not just New York City, but also people across the country and the world?
2. What challenges might airports and authorities face when grounding thousands of flights at the same time?
3. How might it have felt for pilots like Ralph to suddenly be told to land and not take off, especially without knowing why?

CHAPTER FOUR

A TURNING POINT

For Earle, September 11, 2001, is the moment in U.S. history that stands out the most. He worked in the World Trade Center, and that morning, he almost became part of the tragedy himself. The attacks marked a turning point in the lives of thousands of people, from workers in the towers to the families and friends who waited for news, and even to those watching the events unfold from home.

Earle's story shows how close ordinary life and disaster can be, and how the choices and timing of that morning affected people in ways that would last a lifetime.

NARROWLY AVOIDING DISASTER

The day nearly started like any other for Earle. He was getting ready to go to work at the World Trade Center, but was running late, when the news flashed across the TV:

I was working there, about to go to work, when the news came on the TV [saying], "A plane has crashed into the World Trade Center" ... I was working in building Number 2, that's the one they destroyed. I wasn't there, I

Scan this QR code to watch Earle tell his story of how his life was changed on 9/11.

The remains of part of the World Trade Center are shown here at the 9/11 Memorial and Museum.

hadn't come to work yet. Had I been an hour or [so earlier] ... I'd have been in the midst of it ... I was on the 35th floor.

FAST FACT

MORE THAN 430 BUILDINGS IN LOWER MANHATTAN WERE DAMAGED BY DEBRIS, DUST, OR FIRES AFTER THE TWIN TOWERS COLLAPSED.

For many people in New York City, life that morning was full of uncertainty and fear. Some had been rushing to work, others were still at home, and now almost no one knew what to do next.

By 9:59 a.m., the South Tower had collapsed, followed by the North Tower at 10:28 a.m. Even though the South Tower was the second tower to be hit, it collapsed first because the plane crashed into it at a higher speed. Fires burned in surrounding buildings, and thousands of first responders were risking their lives to save others.

The outside of part of the tower ruins are shown here.

FAST FACT

SUBWAYS, BUSES, AND TUNNELS IN LOWER MANHATTAN WERE SHUT DOWN, LEAVING TENS OF THOUSANDS OF COMMUTERS STRANDED FOR HOURS.

LIVING WITH FEAR AND CAUTION

Even though Earle avoided the worst of the disaster, the day left a lasting impression on him. The attacks made him more cautious, aware that even ordinary situations could turn dangerous:

I was very leery about things that were taking place that you thought might develop into a big explosion of some sort. All I did was be careful and watch what I was doing, watch what I said, and watch who I was dealing with.

The human impact was immediate and emotional. Families were left waiting, uncertain if their loved ones were okay, millions of people were stranded, and New Yorkers were forced to rethink how they interacted with their city. Many people who escaped the towers or were nearby found themselves living with a new sense of **vulnerability**. Thousands of people developed long-term health problems from dust and debris, as well as serious mental health problems from the trauma they experienced.

First responders are shown here clearing rubble and searching through the ruins for survivors. Many first responders would later experience physical and mental health problems due to 9/11.

Many people volunteered to help with cleanup efforts after the buildings collapsed.

SAFETY AFTER 9/11

The attacks on 9/11 changed how people work and travel and how cities plan for emergencies. Many office buildings added new safety rules to protect workers in case of future disasters.

One major change was the creation of regular evacuation drills. Many workplaces, especially tall office buildings, now practice what to do in emergencies so people know how to leave safely. Building managers also added emergency supplies, such as first-aid kits, water, and flashlights, to help employees if they are stuck inside during a crisis.

Security rules became stricter, too. Access to some office buildings is now controlled with ID cards or security checkpoints. Visitors often need to check in and wear badges. Some companies even use cameras and monitoring systems to keep track of entrances and hallways.

Emergency communication has also improved. Companies now have plans to alert workers by phone, text, or email if something dangerous is happening. Many offices also create buddy systems or checklists so employees can account for everyone during an emergency.

Air travel also became much stricter after 9/11. Passengers now go through thorough screenings before boarding a flight. Shoes, belts, and liquids are checked carefully, and carry-on items are scanned for dangerous objects. Airport security officers use metal detectors, X-ray machines, and sometimes body scanners to keep flights safe. Pilots are trained to handle emergencies, and reinforced cockpit doors help prevent unauthorized access. Air marshals now sometimes fly on commercial planes to provide extra protection.

The attacks also inspired new security measures across the world.

FAST FACT

THOUSANDS OF VOLUNTEERS CAME TO NEW YORK CITY TO HELP WITH CLEANUP, AID SURVIVORS, AND PROVIDE FOOD, WATER, AND SUPPORT.

LASTING IMPACT

For Earle, and for countless others, 9/11 was a turning point in how they viewed life. It was a reminder that ordinary days and routines could be interrupted. Americans suddenly became aware of the fact that safety was

World Trade Center Building 6, which was next to the North Tower, was severely damaged in the collapse of the towers.

The World Financial Center was severely damaged when the towers collapsed.

The 9/11 attacks changed life forever. President George W. Bush and First Lady Laura Bush are shown here visiting the World Trade Center site in 2006.

not guaranteed and the United States was not immune to acts of shocking, large-scale violence.

The emotional impact lasted for years. Communities came together to support those directly affected, memorials were created to honor the dead, and the nation began a long process of healing. Earle's vigilance and careful observation highlight one way people responded to 9/11: with awareness, caution, and an appreciation for every day that followed.

HOW YOU SEE HISTORY

1. Why do you think 9/11 is considered such a turning point in U.S. history?
2. How do you think the attacks affect people who were far away from New York City but still witnessed the events on TV?
3. Talk to a trusted adult you know who was alive on 9/11. What are their memories of how they felt that day and afterward?

CHAPTER FIVE

FAMILIES AND FRIENDS LEFT WAITING

For thousands of families, the morning began with worry and confusion. People didn't know if their loved ones had survived, and answers didn't come for days. The human impact of the attacks went far beyond the collapse of the towers.

In David's interview, he recalls the sudden silence that hit companies like Cantor Fitzgerald, whose employees worked at the top of the Twin Towers. Families and coworkers couldn't reach their friends, and the shock of not knowing who had survived was overwhelming.

THE ABSENCE OF PHONE CALLS

Phones that were usually busy with calls from coworkers, friends, and loved ones suddenly went silent. Offices, like those of Cantor Fitzgerald at the top of the towers, went completely quiet. In an interview, David remembered stories from people trying to reach their coworkers in the Twin Towers:

One of the big firms that was hurt the most was Cantor Fitzgerald in the World Trade Center. And when I came here [to Dallas, Texas] to work for High Side, the big hedge fund that I was with, we dealt with

Scan this QR code to watch David talk about friends that were lost on 9/11.

Cantor and hearing their experiences, trying to call people that day.

[Their headquarters] was at the top of the World Trade Center. They [some employees] were here in Dallas and all their traders were there [in New York]. They had no calls to make, they had customers who wanted to do trades at

FAST FACT

THE 9/11 MEMORIAL AND MUSEUM IS FILLED WITH MORE THAN 82,000 ARTIFACTS FROM THE DAY OF THE ATTACKS, INCLUDING RECOVERED STEEL, PERSONAL ITEMS OF THOSE WHO WERE LOST, AND CRUSHED FIRE TRUCKS THAT WERE PULLED OUT OF THE WRECKAGE.

Many pieces that were pulled from the ruins of the towers are now in the 9/11 Memorial and Museum for people to view and remember the events of the day. An elevator motor from one of the towers is shown here.

After the attacks, families posted pictures of missing loved ones with information on how to reach them if found.

First responders are shown helping with cleanup and recovery efforts. Many of their colleagues did not survive.

business, but they were all their friends. So here they are talking to them all day long on the phone every single day, and all of a sudden, nothing. Nine o'clock that morning, there were no more phone calls ... That was it. And they never saw those people again.

Being suddenly unable to reach loved ones, friends, or coworkers that people talked with everyday was one of the first and most painful signs of the human impact of 9/11. People across the city **frantically** tried to find out if their loved ones were safe. Families waited by phones, but there were often no calls or emails to know if someone had made it out of the towers.

SURVIVOR STORIES

Survivors of the attacks on the World Trade Center towers went through incredible lengths to get out of harm's way. Here are a few of their stories.

Marcy Borders: She is commonly known as "The Dust Lady." She worked on the 81st floor in the North Tower. Right after the plane hit, she walked down 81 flights of stairs to escape. A famous picture of her shows her completely covered in thick, gray dust. She died in 2015 from cancer. She believed the toxic dust she inhaled during the attacks caused her cancer.

Joanne Capestro: She worked on the 87th floor of the North Tower. When the plane hit, she felt a very large jolt that pushed her out of her seat. In addition to this, she smelled jet fuel, and ceiling tiles on her floor were falling. She immediately headed for the exit with some coworkers but got separated from them in the stairwell because she got stuck. Civilians were staying on the right side of the stairs when descending to allow first responders and their heavy equipment to come up the stairs on the other side. Throughout her descent, she experienced uncomfortable levels of heat and the smell of gas, but she powered through this, eventually reaching street level right as the South Tower collapsed. This created a large debris cloud and led to a famous picture of her caked in dust.

Lauren Manning: She worked in the North Tower and had just arrived in the lobby when the first plane hit. She was struck by a fireball and flung toward the doors but made it outside to roll on the ground and put out the flames. She was burned on more than 82 percent of her body and had a very low chance of survival. After several months of recovery and dozens of surgeries, she survived and is an inspirational speaker.

POSTERS, PHOTOS, AND SEARCH EFFORTS

In the days following the attacks, **desperate** families and friends posted flyers, photos, and missing-person notices all over New York City. Offices, subway stations, and public spaces were covered with faces of people who hadn't been seen since the morning of the attacks.

Community centers, churches, and schools became gathering places for families seeking information. Volunteers helped distribute flyers, assisted with searches, and offered

One World Trade Center was rebuilt on the World Trade Center Complex.

The 9/11 Memorial has two pools where the towers once stood, with names of those who died stamped into the edges. One of the pools is shown here.

> **FAST FACT**
>
> THE 9/11 MEMORIAL CONSISTS OF TWO POOLS: ONE WHERE THE NORTH TOWER STOOD, AND ONE WHERE THE SOUTH TOWER STOOD. THE OUTSIDE OF EACH POOL IS STAMPED WITH THE NAMES OF THOSE WHO DIED.

emotional support. Some people walked the streets for hours, checking hospitals, shelters, and temporary aid stations to search for news about missing loved ones.

Unfortunately, many of the posters became permanent reminders of lives lost that day. These images, which filled the city, reflected not just the scale of the disaster, but the heartbreak experienced by the thousands of people who were left behind.

THE AFTERMATH OF 9/11

The attacks of September 11, 2001, left a permanent mark on New York City, the United States, and the world. The destruction of the Twin Towers and surrounding buildings, as well as the crashes at the Pentagon and in Pennsylvania, caused an enormous loss of life—nearly 3,000 people died that day. Thousands more were injured or exposed to toxic dust, which led to long-term health problems.

In the weeks and months after the attacks, the country came together in many ways. Emergency responders, volunteers, and neighbors helped clear debris, provide aid, and comfort families. Memorials and shrines appeared spontaneously, with flowers, candles, flags, and photos of the missing. People also contributed to funds that helped victims' families, first responders, and survivors.

FAST FACT

ONE WORLD TRADE CENTER, ALSO KNOWN AS THE FREEDOM TOWER, IS THE TALLEST BUILDING IN THE UNITED STATES. IT'S ONE OF THE BUILDINGS ON THE SITE OF THE TWIN TOWERS.

After the attacks, people left flowers and flags on the fence around the ruins.

Thousands of people lost their lives on 9/11. A wall with some of their photos is shown here in a memorial.

Cleanup and reconstruction in the area took years. This is the progress that was made seven years later, in 2008.

Some Americans, however, did not benefit from this spirit of togetherness and patriotism. One of the painful effects of 9/11 was an increase in discrimination against Mulsims, even though the vast majority of Muslims did not support the actions of the Islamist extremist hijackers.

The attacks also led to long-term changes in safety and emergency preparedness. Airports introduced new safety measures, including enhanced screenings and reinforced cockpit doors.

In Lower Manhattan, the rebuilding process became a symbol of resilience. A national memorial and museum was constructed to honor the victims and preserve their stories for generations to come.

HOW YOU SEE HISTORY

1. Why do you think creating memorials, like the 9/11 Memorial and Museum, is important?
2. Why do you think Islamophobia increased after 9/11?
3. In what ways did the attacks change how Americans view safety in public spaces and on forms of transportation?

The 9/11 Memorial and Museum has a wall with a blue square for each person who passed away in the towers.

TIMELINE

IT BEGAN LIKE ANY OTHER DAY: TIMELINE OF 9/11

- **8:46 a.m.:** American Airlines Flight 11 crashes into the World Trade Center North Tower.
- **8:48 a.m:** Live news coverage starts showing the scene at the World Trade Center.
- **9:03 a.m.:** United Airlines Flight 175 crashes into the World Trade Center South Tower.
- **9:05 a.m.:** President George W. Bush is told about the attacks on the World Trade Center.
- **9:55 a.m.:** President George W. Bush takes off on Air Force One to New York City.

CHAOS AND LOSS: TIMELINE OF 9/11

- **9:37 a.m.:** American Airlines Flight 77 crashes into the Pentagon in Arlington, Virginia.
- **10:02 a.m.:** United Airlines Flight 93 crashes into an empty field in Shanksville, Pennsylvania.

AIR TRAVEL COMES TO A HALT: TIMELINE OF 9/11

- **9:06 a.m.:** Airspace around New York City is shut down.
- **9:45 a.m.:** Airspace is shut down across the entire United States.

A TURNING POINT: TIMELINE OF 9/11

- **9:59 a.m.:** The South Tower collapses.
- **10:28 a.m.:** The North Tower collapses.

GLOSSARY

anxiety: A mental condition marked by strong feelings of fear or nervousness about what might happen.
debris: Broken pieces of objects or objects left somewhere because they are not wanted.
depression: A mental health condition in which a person feels very sad, hopeless, and unimportant and is often unable to do basic tasks because of this.
desperate: Taking an action because of feeling a lot of need to do something.
disbelief: Inability to accept something as real or true.
discriminate: To treat people unequally based on class, race, or religion.
evacuate: To leave, especially from a dangerous area.
expose: To make open to an action or influence.
extremist: A person who believes in or supports ideas that are very far from what people consider correct or reasonable.
frantic: Done very fast and nervously.
hijack: To stop, steal, and take control of something.
navigate: To find one's way.
palpable: Easily seen and able to be touched or felt.
particle: A very small piece of something.
post-traumatic stress disorder (PTSD): A disorder that develops after a very stressful event. People often have flashbacks of the event, anxiety, depression, and nightmares, and avoid reminders of the event.
preserve: To keep safe from destruction and free from decay.
routine: A regular way of doing things in a particular order.
Sikh: A person who follows a certain religion called Sikhism. These people believe that there is one God and all people are equal.
terrorist: A person who uses violent acts to frighten people as a way of trying to achieve a political goal.
threatened: Likely to be harmed.
thwart: To stop something from happening.
vulnerability: Open to being hurt or damaged.

FOR MORE INFORMATION

BOOKS

Blais, Allison. *A Place of Remembrance: Official Book of the National September 11 Memorial*. Washington, DC: National Geographic, 2015.

Bodden, Valerie. *The 9/11 Terror Attacks*. Mankato, MN: Creative Paperbacks, 2016.

Brown, Don. *America Is Under Attack: September 11, 2001: The Day the Towers Fell*. New York City, NY: Roaring Book Press, 2014.

Maranville, Amy. *The 9/11 Terrorist Attacks: A Day That Changed America*. North Mankato, MN: Capstone Press, 2022.

Rubin, Sean. *This Very Tree: A Story of 9/11, Resilience, and Regrowth*. New York City, NY: Henry Holt and Company, 2021.

WEBSITES

9/11 Memorial
www.911memorial.org
Watch videos, explore digital exhibits, learn more about the events of 9/11, and view photos from the day of the attacks and after.

Remembering 9/11
www.archives.gov/news/topics/9-11-anniversary
Watch videos and read more about the attacks on 9/11 at the National Archives.

Remembering September 11
kids.nationalgeographic.com/history/article/remembering-september-11
Read more about the attacks on 9/11 and view pictures of what happened that day.

September 11: A Day of Remembrance and Service
www.nps.gov/subjects/npscelebrates/september-11.htm
Learn more about the 9/11 memorials, view photos, and more.

September 11 Attacks
www.britannica.com/event/September-11-attacks
Read more about the 9/11 attacks with the help of *Encyclopedia Britannica*.

INDEX

PHOTO CREDITS

Cover pp. 12, 14, 15, 20, 25, 26, 28, 29, 40, 48, 49, 53 courtesy of the Libary of Congress; p. 7 Flight paths of hijacked planes-September 11 attacks/Wikimedia Commons; p. 9 Benny Marty/Shutterstock.com; p. 10 2001-was-a-project-by-wolfgangstaehle-e28093-on-8-september-2001-two-cameras-would-automatically-takea-photo-of-the-manhattan-skyline-everyfour-seconds/Wikimedia Commons; p. 11 UA175 Explosion Todd Rengel/Wikimedia Commons; p. 17 Walter Cicchetti/Shutterstock.com; pp. 21, 42 Anthony Correia/Shutterstock.com; p. 22 NYCTA-Miller,G CD1-017/Wikimedia Commons; p. 23 Everett Collection/Shutterstock.com; p. 24 HE Photography/Shutterstock.com; p. 27 Rawpixel.com/Shutterstock.com; p. 30, 47, 55 Pit Stock/Shutterstock.com; p. 31 Kenneth Summers/Shutterstock.com; p. 33 World Trade Center Site After 9-11 Attacks With Original Building Locations/Wikimedia Commons; p 34 mrtravelbunny/Shutterstock.com; p. 35 Frank Wagner/Shutterstock.com; p 36 Howard Weiss/Shutterstock.com; p. 39 Henk Vrieselaar/Shutterstock.com; p. 41 FEMA - 3922 - Photograph by Andrea Booher taken on 09-16-2001 in New York/Wikimedia Commons; p. 44 (top) World Trade Center Photos (6120692530)/Wikimedia Commons; p. 44 (bottom) World Financial Center Sept. 14, 2001/Wikimedia Commons; p. 45 President George W. Bush and Laura Bush look over the World Trade Center site Sunday, September 10, 2006/Wikimedia Commons; p. 51 Marcoss/Shutterstock.com; p. 52 Wlin001/Shutterstock.com; p. 54 (top) USAF photo 120820-F-FT240-378 -World Trade Center tour - AFW - Flickr id 7890081590/Wikimedia Commons; p. 54 (bottom) katuSka/Shutterstock.com.

ABOUT THE AUTHOR

NICOLE HORNING is a published author of several nonfiction books for children and teens. She has her Bachelor's degree in English and a Master's degree in education. She doesn't just write for a living; she also enjoys it as a hobby. Nicole loves to collect books and read anything that sounds interesting to her. She also loves learning new things, especially historical topics. She does her best work while listening to Taylor Swift and having one of her two cats in her lap—both things happen a lot.

She remembers being in school on September 11, watching TV when the second plane hit the South Tower, and then watching the news in class for the rest of the day. After visiting the 9/11 Memorial and Museum, she thinks it's an important site for everyone to experience.